STANDARD OF EXCELLENCE

ENHANCED COMPREHENSIVE BAND METHOD

By Bruce Pearson

Dear Student:

Congratulations! You have successfully attained the first level in achieving a standard of excellence in music-making. By now, you have discovered that careful study and regular practice have brought you the joy and satisfaction of making beautiful music.

You are now ready to move to the next level in your music-making. I want to welcome you to STANDARD OF EXCELLENCE *ENHANCED*, Book 2. I also want to wish you continued success and enjoyment.

Best wishes,

Bruce Pearson

Practice and Assessment - the key to EXCELLENCE!

▶ Make practicing part of your daily schedule. If you plan it as you do any other activity, you will find plenty of time for it.
▶ Try to practice in the same place every day. Choose a place where you can concentrate on making music. Start with a regular and familiar warm-up routine, including long tones and simple technical exercises. Like an athlete, you need to warm-up your mind and muscles before you begin performing.
▶ Always tune before you play. Use the tuning tracks found on the Accompaniment Recordings, or use the *iPAS* Tuner.
▶ Set goals for every practice session. Keep track of your practice time and progress on the front cover Practice Journal.
▶ Practice the difficult spots in your lesson assignment and band music over and over at a slower tempo, until you can play them perfectly, then gradually increase the tempo. Use the *iPAS* Metronome to track your progress and ensure you are playing with a steady pulse.
▶ Spend time practicing alone and with the Accompaniment Recordings.
▶ Assess your progress and achievements by using *iPAS*. Listen to the recordings you create to hear the spots in the music which might need improvement.
▶ At the end of each practice session, play something fun!

ISBN 0-8497-0779-X

kjos NEIL A. KJOS MUSIC COMPANY, PUBLISHER   PW22TB

REVIEW

B♭ MAJOR KEY SIGNATURE

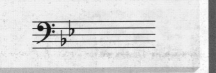

1 WARM-UP - Band Arrangement

Andante

2 B♭ MAJOR SCALE SKILL

Moderato   Arpeggio   Chords   div.

► Lines with a medal are *Achievement Lines.* The chart on page 47 can be used to record your progress.

3 BOTANY BAY   **Page 40** ▶   Australian Folk Song

Moderato

► When you see a page number followed by an arrow, *Excellerate* to the page indicated for additional studies.

4 DRIVE TIME

Andante

5 SHEPHERD'S HEY   English Folk Song

Moderato   *Fine*

D.C. al Fine

REVIEW

**Eb MAJOR
KEY SIGNATURE**

6 Eb MAJOR SCALE SKILL

Moderato

mf

Arpeggio   Chords div.

▶ Are you playing with a good embouchure and hand position?

7 MOLLY MALONE

Irish Folk Song

Andante

mp   *f*   *mp*   *mp*
rit.

8 NO LOOKING BACK   **Page 40** ▍▍▍▶

Moderato

mf

9 TURKISH MARCH

Wolfgang Amadeus Mozart (1756 - 1791)

Allegro

mf

10 HYMN OF THANKSGIVING - Band Arrangement

Johann Crüger (1598 - 1662)
arr. Bruce Pearson (b. 1942)

Andante

mf   *p*   *mf*

p

f   *mf*   *rit.*

REVIEW

F MAJOR KEY SIGNATURE

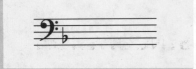

Be a C D F

11 WARM-UP - Band Arrangement

Andante

mf

12 F MAJOR SCALE SKILL

Moderato — Arpeggio — Chords

f 1 4 3 2 1 | 4 3 1 3 4 | 1 2 3 4 1 | 1 3 1 1 3 1 3 4 | 1 | 1 6 1

13 KNUCKLEBUSTER

Moderato

mf 4 1 3 2 4 2 3 4 | 4 3 1 3 1 4 3 2 3 4 1 3 4 6 1 3 1 4 3 4 3 2

1. 2.

4 3 1 3 2 3 4 1 4 1 3 4 3 1 4 2 3 4 1 4 1 3 4 1

14 GIVE ME THAT OLD TIME RELIGION

Page 40 ▌▌▌▌➡

American Spiritual

Allegro

f 1 6 4 1 1 1 4 6 1 1 1 4 4 3 4 1 1 1 4 3 3 3 4 1 4 6 1 4 1

clap

15 _____

Composer _____

your name

Moderato

▶ Compose an ending for this melody. Title and play your composition.

16 FOR TROMBONES ONLY

Page 40 ▌▌▌▌➡

Allegro

mf

SYNCOPATION		A rhythmic effect which places emphasis on a weak or unaccented part of the measure.
INTERVAL		The distance between any two notes.

17 SYNCOPATION SENSATION

18 THE RIDDLE SONG

American Folk Song

► Write in the counting and clap the rhythm before you play.

19 NOBODY KNOWS THE TROUBLE I'VE SEEN

American Spiritual

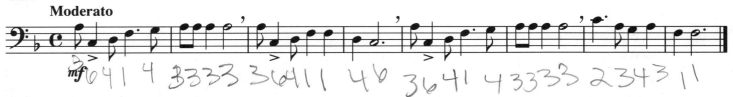

20 INTERVAL INQUIRY

► Sing this exercise using the numbers before you play.

21 GO FOR EXCELLENCE!

American Folk Song

| G MINOR KEY SIGNATURE | | **G minor** has the same key signature as **B♭ major**. |

| **TEMPO** | *Accelerando (accel.)* - Gradually increase the tempo. |

22 **WARM-UP - Band Arrangement**

Andante

mf

23 **G NATURAL MINOR SCALE SKILL**

Moderato

f

24 **G HARMONIC MINOR SCALE SKILL**

Moderato

f

25 **MINKA, MINKA**

Ukrainian Folk Song

Moderato

mp   2nd time - *accel.*   Hey!

26 **LAREDO - Duet**

Mexican Folk Song

Moderato

f

▶ Name the interval between the top and bottom notes of the last measure. _____

27 **TURNING YOU LOOSE**

Moderato

mf

28 **FOR TROMBONES ONLY** Page 40 ▐▐▐▐▐▶

6 alternate   mf

DAL SEGNO AL FINE (D.S. AL FINE)

Go back to the sign (𝄋) and play until the *Fine.*

JOYEUX NOËL
Band Arrangement

French Carol
arr. Chuck Elledge (b. 1961)

29 **GO FOR EXCELLENCE!**

EIGHTH REST

γ

γ = ½ count in $\frac{2}{4}$, $\frac{3}{4}$, and $\frac{4}{4}$ time.

An eighth rest is as long as an eighth note.

30 EIGHTH REST ON THE BEAT

Moderato

mf

▶ Write in the counting and clap the rhythm before you play.

31 EIGHTH REST OFF THE BEAT

Moderato

f

32 ACADEMIC FESTIVAL MARCH - Trio

Johannes Brahms (1833 - 1897)

Moderato

A.   *f*

B.   *f*

C.   *f*

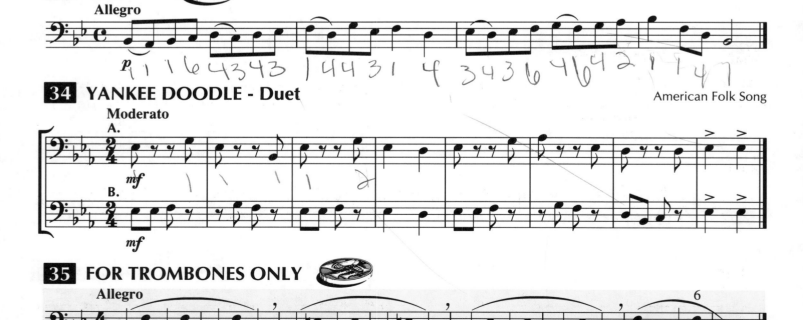

33 BREEZIN'

Allegro

p   1 1 1 6 4 3 4 3 | 4 4 3 1   4   3 4 3 6 4 6 4 2 1 1 4 1

34 YANKEE DOODLE - Duet

American Folk Song

Moderato

A.   *mf*

B.   *mf*

35 FOR TROMBONES ONLY

Allegro

f

Ab MAJOR KEY SIGNATURE	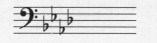	This key signature means play all B's as B flats, all E's as E flats, all A's as A flats, and all D's as D flats.
TEXTURES		**Monophony** - a single unaccompanied melody.
		Polyphony - two or more melodies played at the same time.

36 Ab MAJOR SCALE SKILL

Andante

f

Arpeggio   Chords   div.

37 GREASED LIGHTNING

Allegro

mf

38 PARTNER SONGS - Duet

Moderato
A. *"White Coral Bells"*   Traditional

mf

B. *"Vespers Song"*   Russian Air

mf

▶ For an example of monophony, play line A or line B alone. For an example of polyphony, play line A while someone else plays line B.

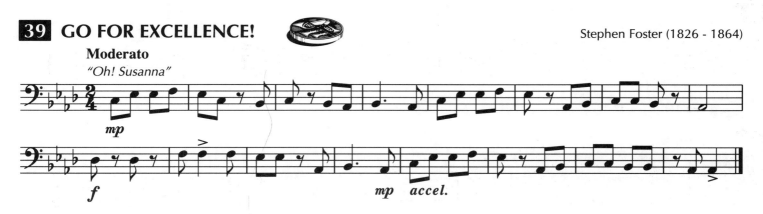

39 GO FOR EXCELLENCE!   Stephen Foster (1826 - 1864)

Moderato
"Oh! Susanna"

mp

f   mp   accel.

ENHARMONICS

F♯ = G♭

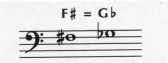

Notes that sound the same but are written differently.

ARTICULATION

Staccato (dot placed above or below note) - Play short and detached.

TEMPO

Allegretto - light and lively; slightly slower than **Allegro.**

---

40 WARM-UP - Band Arrangement

Andante

mf

---

41 CHROMATIC CAPERS

Moderato   G♭

f   enharmonic   enharmonic

---

42 SHENANDOAH   **Page 40** ▐▐▐▐➡   American Folk Song

Andante

mp

---

43 THEME FROM SYMPHONY NO. 94   Franz Joseph Haydn (1732 - 1809)

Andante

p

---

44 PARADE OF THE TIN SOLDIERS   Léon Jessel (1871 - 1942)

Allegretto

mf

---

45 FOR TROMBONES ONLY

Allegro

mf

C MINOR KEY SIGNATURE	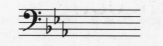	**C minor** has the same key signature as E♭ **major.**
ARTICULATIONS		*Tenuto* (line placed above or below note) - Sustain for full value. *Legato* - Play as smoothly as possible.

46 C NATURAL MINOR SCALE

47 C HARMONIC MINOR SCALE

48 MARCHE SLAV

Peter Ilyich Tchaikovsky (1840 - 1893)

49 GREENSLEEVES

English Song

▶ Name the key in "Greensleeves."

50 JUBILATE

Wolfgang Amadeus Mozart (1756 - 1791)

51 GO FOR EXCELLENCE!

TEXTURE	**Melody and Accompaniment** - main melody is accompanied by chords or less important melodies called **countermelodies**.

52 WARM-UP
Andante
mf legato

53 HABAÑERA
Georges Bizet (1838 - 1875)
Andante
mf

54 SMOOTH AS SILK
Allegretto
f

55 HEY HO - Round (Canon)
Medieval Song
Allegro

56 THE BRITISH GRENADIERS - Duet
English Folk Song
Allegro
A. Melody
f
B. Countermelody
f

57 FOR TROMBONES ONLY
Page 41
Andante
f
alternate

TIME SIGNATURE 𝄵

This time signature is called **cut time** or *alla breve*.

𝄵 = **2** = 2 counts in each measure
2 = half note gets 1 count

58 CUT AND PASTE

Moderato

▶ Write in the counting and clap the rhythm before you play.

59 OATS, PEAS, BEANS

American Folk Song

Moderato

60 THE VICTORS

Fight Song

Allegro

61 OVER EASY

Page 41 ▶

Andante

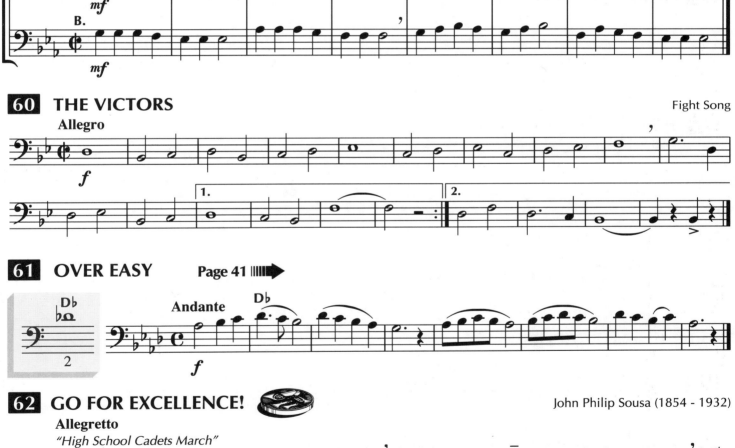

62 GO FOR EXCELLENCE!

John Philip Sousa (1854 - 1932)

Allegretto
"High School Cadets March"

PW22TB

ENHARMONICS

C# = Db

CHORD

fifth
third
root

Two or more pitches sounded
at the same time.

63 WARM-UP - Band Arrangement

Andante   C#

mf

5

64 DANISH ROLL

Danish Folk Song

Moderato   *Fine*

mp

D.C. al Fine

f

65 RUSSIAN SAILORS' DANCE

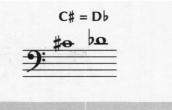

Reinhold Glière (1875 - 1956)

Allegretto

f

Fine

mf

D.C. al Fine

66 CHORD CAPERS

major chord   minor chord

▶ Listen for the different types of chords played by the full band.

67 FOR TROMBONES ONLY

Allegro

mf

ENHARMONICS

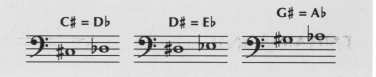

68 CHROMATIC SCALE SKILL

69 SAILING THE HIGH SEAS

70 CHROMATIC MARCH

Page 41

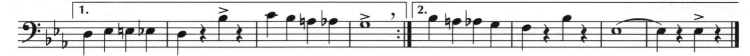

71 MANHATTAN BEACH MARCH

John Philip Sousa (1854 - 1932)

72 GO FOR EXCELLENCE!

▶ Play using each of the following articulations: A. B. C. D.

PW22TB

DA CAPO AL CODA (D.C. AL CODA)

Go back to the beginning and play until the coda sign (⊕). When you reach the coda sign, skip to the *Coda* (⊕).

ROCK ISLAND EXPRESS
Band Arrangement

Chuck Elledge (b. 1961)

TIME SIGNATURE

$\frac{3}{8}$

3 = 3 counts in each measure
8 = eighth note gets 1 count

73 _____   Composer _____

your name

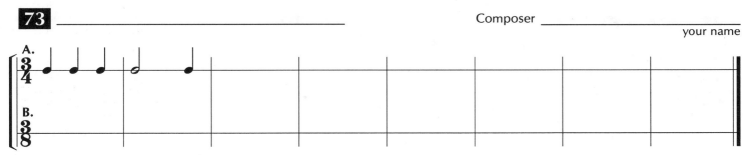

▶ Compose an ending for the $\frac{3}{4}$ rhythm composition on line **A**. Title your composition, then count and clap it.

▶ On line **B**, rewrite your composition in $\frac{3}{8}$. Count and clap it.

74 **TRIPLE PLAY**

Allegretto

▶ Write in the counting and clap the rhythm before you play.

75 **WE THREE KINGS**   Page 41 ▏▏▏▶   John H. Hopkins, Jr. (1820 - 1891)

Andante

▶ Name the key in "We Three Kings." _____

76 **GO FOR EXCELLENCE!**

Allegro

C MAJOR KEY SIGNATURE

This key signature contains no sharps or flats.

TIME SIGNATURE

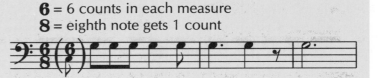

6 = 6 counts in each measure
8 = eighth note gets 1 count

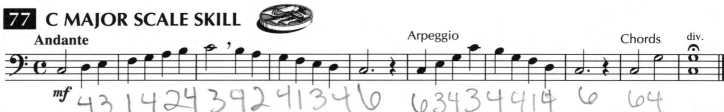

77 C MAJOR SCALE SKILL

Andante Arpeggio Chords div.

mf 43142439241346 63434414 6 64

78 OVER THE RIVER

Traditional

Allegro 1.

2.

▶ Draw in a breath mark at the end of each phrase.

79 OODLES OF NOODLES

Moderato

80 UPS AND DOWNS

Allegretto

▶ Write in the counting and draw in the bar lines before you play.

81 FOR TROMBONES ONLY

Allegro

88 LOOBY LOO

Anonymous

▶ Name the key in "Looby Loo." _____

89 THE THUNDERER

John Philip Sousa (1854 - 1932)

90 LISTEN TO THE MOCKINGBIRD

Alice Hawthorne (1827 - 1902)

91 GIVE MY REGARDS TO BROADWAY

George M. Cohan (1878 - 1942)

92 FOR TROMBONES ONLY

Page 41 ▷▷▷

EIGHTH/SIXTEENTH NOTE COMBINATIONS

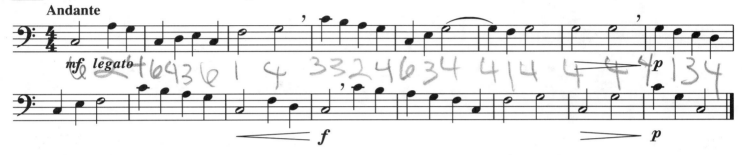

93 **CHESTER - Band Arrangement**

William Billings (1746 - 1800)
arr. Bruce Pearson (b. 1942)

Andante

94 **STEADY AS YOU GO - Duet**

Moderato

95 **TIRRA LIRRA LOO**

Canadian Folk Song

Moderato

▶ Write in the counting and clap the rhythm before you play.

96 **GO FOR EXCELLENCE!**

American Folk Song

Moderato

"Big Rock Candy Mountain"

The written piano accompaniment for TURKISH MARCH is included on track 1 of CD 2 for easy access in a performance situation.

TURKISH MARCH
from "The Ruins of Athens"
Solo with Piano Accompaniment

Ludwig van Beethoven (1770 - 1827)
arr. Bruce Pearson (b. 1942)

97 BLAZIN'

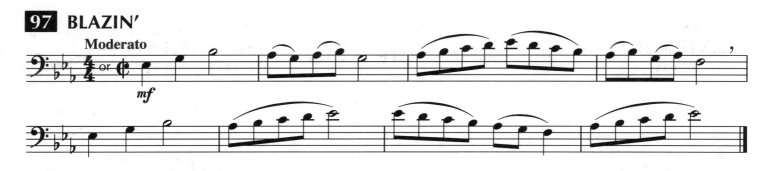

▶ Name the interval between the first and second notes. _____

98 AMERICAN PATROL

Frank W. Meacham (1856 - 1909)

99 KERRY DANCE

Page 41 ▷

Irish Folk Song

100 GAVOTTE

James Hook (1746 - 1827)

101 FOR TROMBONES ONLY

SINGLE SIXTEENTH NOTE		DOTTED EIGHTH NOTE		DOTTED EIGHTH/ SIXTEENTH NOTE COMBINATION	

A single sixteenth note is half as long as an eighth note.

♪ = ¼ count in 𝄴, 𝄵, and 𝄵 time.

A dot after a note adds half the value of the note.

♪ + · = ♪ + ♪ = ♪·

102 DOTS OF FUN

Moderato

103 LITTLE BROWN JUG - Duet

Joseph Eastburn Winner (1837 - 1918)

Allegro

▶ Write in the counting and clap the rhythm before you play.

104 OUR BOYS WILL SHINE TONIGHT

College Song

Allegretto

▶ Draw in a breath mark at the end of each phrase.

105 _____ Composer _____
your name

▶ Compose an ending for this melody. Be sure to use the ♪·♪ rhythm. Title and play your composition.

106 GO FOR EXCELLENCE!

Georges Bizet (1838 - 1875)

Allegro

"Farandole from L'Arlesienne Suite"

107 CUCKOO SONG Page 41 ▶ Austrian Folk Song

108 MARCH MILITAIRE Franz Schubert (1797 - 1828)

109 ST. ANTHONY CHORALE Franz Joseph Haydn (1732 - 1809)

110 _____ Composer _____
your name

▶ Arrange these melodic pieces in any order to build a tune you like. You may use pieces more than once. Title and play your composition.

111 FOR TROMBONES ONLY

▶ Play each of the lip slur patterns using the following slide positions: **1; 2; 3; 4; 5; 6; 7.**
You will be moving down a half step with each position.

EIGHTH NOTE TRIPLET

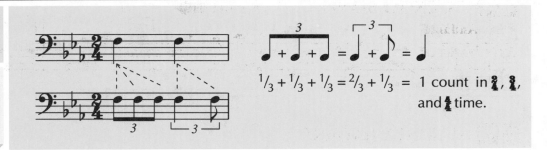

$$\frac{1}{3} + \frac{1}{3} + \frac{1}{3} = \frac{2}{3} + \frac{1}{3} = 1 \text{ count in } \frac{2}{2}, \frac{3}{2}, \text{ and } \frac{4}{4} \text{ time.}$$

TEMPO

Maestoso - majestically

112 TRIPLE TREAT

Moderato

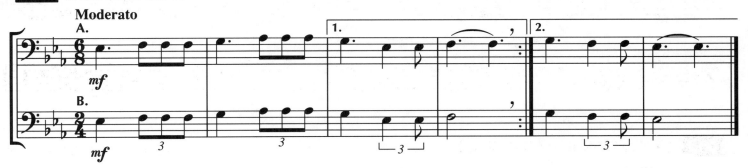

113 STARS OF THE HEAVENS - Duet

Page 41 ▶

Mexican Folk Song

Allegro

114 LIGHT CAVALRY OVERTURE

Franz von Suppé (1819 - 1895)

Maestoso

115 GO FOR EXCELLENCE!

Charles Gounod (1818 - 1893)

Maestoso

"Soldiers' Chorus from Faust"

PW22TB

116 HERE WE COME A-WASSAILING  English Folk Song

117 THEME FROM "ZAMPA" Ferdinand Herold (1791 - 1833)

118 GO FOR EXCELLENCE! Peter Ilyich Tchaikovsky (1840 - 1893)

CABO RICO

Band Arrangement

Chuck Elledge (b. 1961)

PW22TB

RUDIMENTAL REGIMENT
Band Arrangement

Bruce Pearson (b. 1942)
and Chuck Elledge (b. 1961)

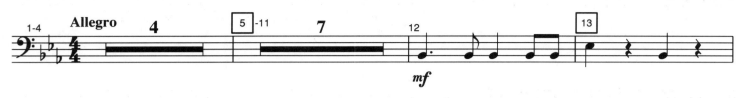

PW22TB

SUMMER'S RAIN

Band Arrangement

Chuck Elledge (b. 1961)

FRENCH MARKET BUZZARDS MARCH
Band Arrangement

Liberato Gallo
arr. Wendy Barden (b. 1955)

ROMANZA
Ensemble

Trombone

Ludwig van Beethoven, Op. 40 (1770 - 1827)
arr. Janice Strobl Kersey (b. 1959)

HORNPIPE from "Water Music"

Ensemble

George Frideric Handel (1685 - 1759)
arr. Janice Strobl Kersey (b. 1959)

Trombone

mf - 1st time
f - 2nd time

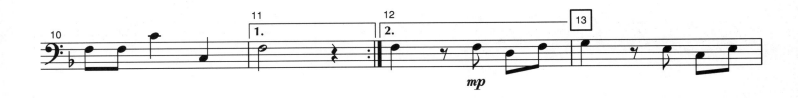

PW22TB

The written piano accompaniment for MINUET and BOURRÉE is included on tracks 11 and 12 of CD 2. You will hear a 2-measure click before you play to help you get started.

MINUET AND BOURRÉE
Solo with Piano Accompaniment
Minuet

George Frideric Handel (1685 - 1759)
arr. Bruce Pearson (b. 1942)

Bourrée

EXCELLERATORS-FOR TROMBONES ONLY

EXCELLERATORS - FOR TROMBONES ONLY

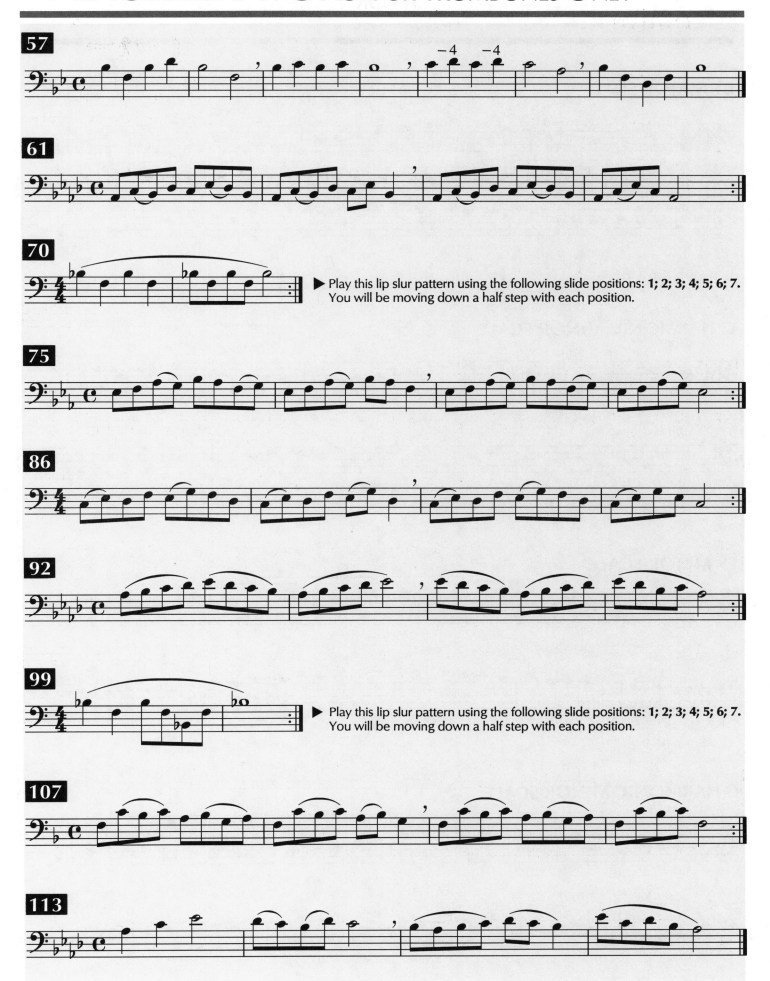

70 ▶ Play this lip slur pattern using the following slide positions: **1; 2; 3; 4; 5; 6; 7.** You will be moving down a half step with each position.

99 ▶ Play this lip slur pattern using the following slide positions: **1; 2; 3; 4; 5; 6; 7.** You will be moving down a half step with each position.

SCALE STUDIES

B♭ MAJOR SCALE

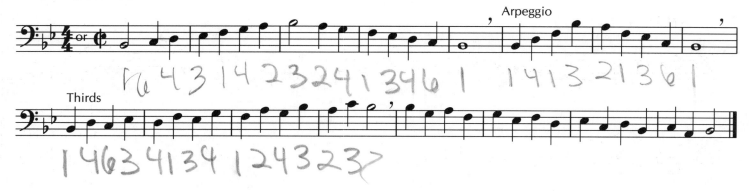

G HARMONIC MINOR SCALE

E♭ MAJOR SCALE

C HARMONIC MINOR SCALE

SCALE STUDIES

F MAJOR SCALE

Ab MAJOR SCALE

C MAJOR SCALE

CHROMATIC SCALE

RHYTHM STUDIES

RHYTHM STUDIES

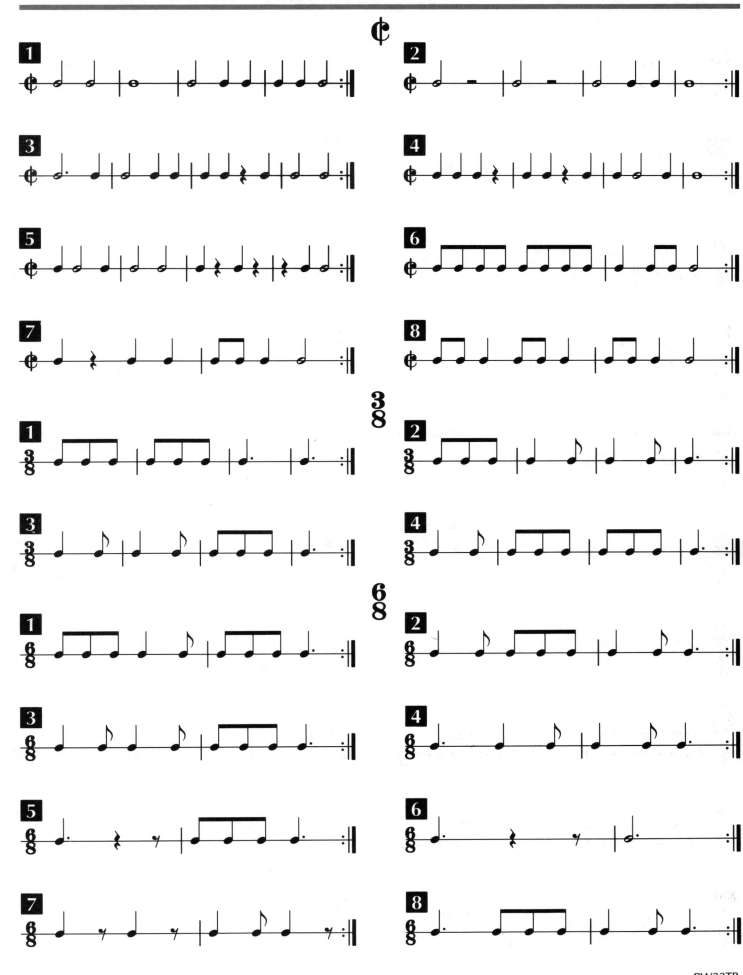

GLOSSARY/INDEX

STANDARD OF EXCELLENCE

EXERCISE 2
- [ ] notes/rhythm
- [ ] posture
- [ ] embouchure
- [ ] breathing

EXERCISE 5
- [ ] notes/rhythm
- [ ] dynamics
- [ ] articulations
- [ ] *D. C. al Fine*

EXERCISE 6
- [ ] notes/rhythm
- [ ] hand position
- [ ] breathing
- [ ] tone

EXERCISE 7
- [ ] notes/rhythm
- [ ] *ritardando*
- [ ] dynamics
- [ ] 1st/2nd endings

EXERCISE 12
- [ ] notes/rhythm
- [ ] posture
- [ ] hand position
- [ ] breathing

EXERCISE 16
- [ ] notes/rhythm
- [ ] embouchure
- [ ] hand position
- [ ] tone

EXERCISE 21
- [ ] notes/rhythm
- [ ] hand position
- [ ] dynamics
- [ ] tempo

EXERCISE 24
- [ ] notes/rhythm
- [ ] embouchure
- [ ] (fermata)
- [ ] tone

EXERCISE 28
- [ ] notes/rhythm
- [ ] posture
- [ ] hand position
- [ ] tone

EXERCISE 29
- [ ] notes/rhythm
- [ ] embouchure
- [ ] breathing
- [ ] *D. C. al Fine*

EXERCISE 33
- [ ] notes/rhythm
- [ ] hand position
- [ ] dynamics
- [ ] tone

EXERCISE 35
- [ ] notes/rhythm
- [ ] breathing
- [ ] tempo
- [ ] tone

EXERCISE 36
- [ ] notes/rhythm
- [ ] posture
- [ ] embouchure
- [ ] tone

EXERCISE 39
- [ ] notes/rhythm
- [ ] embouchure
- [ ] dynamics
- [ ] *accelerando*

EXERCISE 42
- [ ] notes/rhythm
- [ ] hand position
- [ ] time signatures
- [ ] (fermata)

EXERCISE 45
- [ ] notes/rhythm
- [ ] hand position
- [ ] articulation
- [ ] tone

EXERCISE 47
- [ ] notes/rhythm
- [ ] posture
- [ ] tenuto
- [ ] tone

EXERCISE 51
- [ ] notes/rhythm
- [ ] hand position
- [ ] articulation
- [ ] tempo

EXERCISE 53
- [ ] notes/rhythm
- [ ] embouchure
- [ ] accents
- [ ] tempo

EXERCISE 57
- [ ] notes/rhythm
- [ ] hand position
- [ ] embouchure
- [ ] tone

EXERCISE 62
- [ ] notes/rhythm
- [ ] dynamics
- [ ] tenuto
- [ ] tempo

EXERCISE 65
- [ ] notes/rhythm
- [ ] posture
- [ ] articulations
- [ ] *D. C. al Fine*

EXERCISE 67
- [ ] notes/rhythm
- [ ] hand position
- [ ] embouchure
- [ ] tone

EXERCISE 69
- [ ] notes/rhythm
- [ ] hand position
- [ ] embouchure
- [ ] tone

EXERCISE 72
- [ ] notes/rhythm
- [ ] posture
- [ ] articulations
- [ ] breathing

EXERCISE 76
- [ ] notes/rhythm
- [ ] tempo
- [ ] legato
- [ ] tone

EXERCISE 77
- [ ] notes/rhythm
- [ ] hand position
- [ ] tempo
- [ ] tone

EXERCISE 81
- [ ] notes/rhythm
- [ ] hand position
- [ ] embouchure
- [ ] tone

EXERCISE 87
- [ ] notes/rhythm
- [ ] dynamics
- [ ] tone
- [ ] tempo

EXERCISE 88
- [ ] notes/rhythm
- [ ] hand position
- [ ] time signatures
- [ ] tonguing

EXERCISE 91
- [ ] notes/rhythm
- [ ] *D. C. al Coda*
- [ ] tempo
- [ ] tone

EXERCISE 92
- [ ] notes/rhythm
- [ ] hand position
- [ ] posture
- [ ] tone

EXERCISE 96
- [ ] notes/rhythm
- [ ] dynamics
- [ ] accents
- [ ] tonguing

EXERCISE 100
- [ ] notes/rhythm
- [ ] dynamics
- [ ] articulations
- [ ] tempo

EXERCISE 101
- [ ] notes/rhythm
- [ ] hand position
- [ ] posture
- [ ] tone

EXERCISE 106
- [ ] notes/rhythm
- [ ] accents
- [ ] tempo
- [ ] tone

EXERCISE 111
- [ ] notes/rhythm
- [ ] tempo
- [ ] posture
- [ ] tone

EXERCISE 115
- [ ] notes/rhythm
- [ ] hand position
- [ ] tempo
- [ ] accents

EXERCISE 116
- [ ] notes/rhythm
- [ ] time signatures
- [ ] tempo
- [ ] articulations

EXERCISE 118
- [ ] notes/rhythm
- [ ] articulations
- [ ] tempo
- [ ] tone

EXCELLENCE

THE TROMBONE

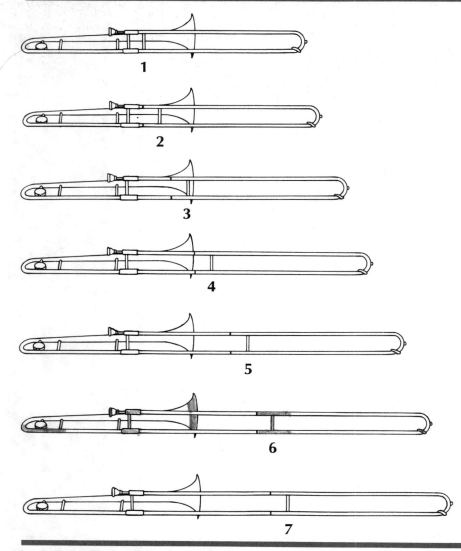

1

2

3

4

5

6

7

TROMBONE CHECKLIST

☐ Sitting up straight

☐ Head erect

☐ Left hand and wrist position correct

☐ Right hand and wrist position correct

☐ Trombone correctly positioned in relation to body

☐ Fingers gently curved

☐ Elbows away from body

☐ Proper mouthpiece placement

☐ Corners of lips firm and center relax

☐ Chin flat and pointed

☐ Breathing properly

☐ Relaxed buzz

TROMBONE SURVIVAL KIT

☐ soft, clean cloth

☐ slide oil

☐ mutes

☐ method book

☐ music stand

☐ mouthpiece cleaning brush

☐ tuning slide grease

☐ pencil

☐ band music